USING THIS BOOK

*One of the best ways of helping children to learn to read is by reading stories to them and with them. This way they learn what **reading** is, and they will gradually come to recognise many words, and begin to read for themselves.*

First, grown-ups read the story on the left-hand pages aloud to the child.

You can reread the story as often as the child enjoys hearing it. Talk about the pictures as you go.

Later the child will read the words under the pictures on the right-hand page.

The pages at the back of the book will give you some ideas for helping your child to read.

British Library Cataloguing in Publication Data

McCullagh, Sheila K.
    The tale of a tail. —(Puddle Lane. Series no. 855. Stage 1; v. 9)
    1. Readers—1950-
    I. Title   II. Dillow, John   III. Series
    428.6   PE1119
    ISBN 0-7214-0916-4

First edition

Published by Ladybird Books Ltd Loughborough Leicestershire UK
Ladybird Books Inc Lewiston Maine 04240 USA

© Text and layout SHEILA McCULLAGH MCMLXXXV
© In publication LADYBIRD BOOKS LTD MCMLXXXV

The tale of a tail

written by SHEILA McCULLAGH
illustrated by JOHN DILLOW

This book belongs to:

Ladybird Books

Sarah lived in Puddle Lane.
She had a strange friend,
called the Griffle.
The Griffle was a green monster.
He could vanish
whenever he wanted to.
The Griffle had long green ears.
He had big green eyes,
and a long green tail.
This is a story about
the Griffle's tail,
and what happened
when somebody pulled it.

Sarah

Mrs Pitter-Patter
lived in Puddle Lane.
(Mrs Pitter-Patter always made
a great deal of noise, and
she was always asking questions.)

Mrs Pitter-Patter

One day, when she was
outside in the lane,
Mrs Pitter-Patter saw Sarah.
Sarah was playing hide and seek
with the Griffle.
(The Griffle could vanish
when he wanted to,
so he was very good at hiding.)

Mrs Pitter-Patter
saw Sarah.

"What **are** you doing, Sarah?"
asked Mrs Pitter-Patter.
"I'm playing with my friend,"
said Sarah.
"What friend?"
asked Mrs Pitter-Patter.
"I'm playing with my friend
the Griffle," said Sarah.
"What Griffle?"
asked Mrs Pitter-Patter.
"**I** can't see anyone."

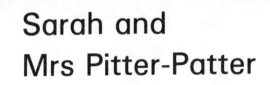

Sarah and
Mrs Pitter-Patter

"Look," said Sarah.

"If you look very hard,

you can see the Griffle's ears."

"What ears?" said Mrs Pitter-Patter.

"I can only see two green leaves."

"Look," said Sarah.

"Look," said Sarah.
"If you look very hard,
you can see the Griffle's eyes."
"What eyes?" asked Mrs Pitter-Patter.
"I can only see two green flowers."

"Look," said Sarah.

"Look," said Sarah.
"If you look a little harder,
you can see the Griffle's tail."
"What tail?" asked Mrs Pitter-Patter.
"I can't see any tail."

"Look," said Sarah.

The Griffle's green tail
was hanging over the wall.
Mrs Pitter-Patter saw it.
"That's a green rope,"
said Mrs Pitter-Patter.
"But it isn't a rope," said Sarah.
"It's the Griffle's tail."
"Of course it's a rope,"
said Mrs Pitter-Patter.
"I shall pull it down!"
She took hold of the Griffle's tail,
and gave a long, hard pull.

Mrs Pitter-Patter
pulled the Griffle's
green tail.

The Griffle jumped down from the wall
with a roar!
The whole of the Griffle was there.
You could see every bit of him.

The Griffle jumped
down from the wall.

Mrs Pitter-Patter
dropped the tail with a yell.
She made such a noise,
that she woke Mr Gotobed,
who was fast asleep in bed
in the house at the end
of the lane.

Mr Gotobed woke up.

Mr Gotobed jumped out of bed,
and ran to the window.
He threw up the window,
and looked out into the lane.
The Griffle had vanished again,
but he saw Mrs Pitter-Patter.

Mr Gotobed looked
out of the window.

Mrs Pitter-Patter ran away.
"What was that?" cried Mr Gotobed.
"What's happened?
Where are you running to,
Mrs Pitter-Patter?"
Mrs Pitter-Patter was running
so fast down the lane,
that she didn't hear
what Mr Gotobed said.
She didn't even see him.

Mrs Pitter-Patter
ran away.

Mrs Pitter-Patter reached
her own door.
She ran into the house,
and shut the door behind her
with a bang!

Mrs Pitter-Patter
ran into the house.

Mr Gotobed shook his head.
"What a noise
Mrs Pitter-Patter makes!"
he said.
"And at this time of day, too!
Just when I'd got to sleep."
Mr Gotobed shut his window
and went back to bed.

Mr Gotobed
went back to bed.

"Where are you, Griffle?"
asked Sarah.
Sarah saw two green ears,
poking up over the wall.
"Has she gone?" asked the Griffle.
He spoke very softly,
in a whiffly-griffly voice.

Sarah saw
two green ears.

"Yes, she's gone," said Sarah.
"Please come back and play."
Two green eyes appeared,
under the green ears.
The Griffle looked down the lane.

The Griffle looked
down the lane.

"I think I'll come another day,
when **she** isn't about,"
he said.
The ears and the eyes disappeared,
and Sarah went home.

Sarah went home.

Notes for the parent/teacher

When you have read the story, go back to the beginning. Look at each picture and talk about it, pointing to the caption below, and reading it aloud yourself.

Run your finger along under the words as you read, so that the child learns that reading goes from left to right. (You needn't say this in so many words. Children learn many useful things about reading by just reading with you, and it is often better to let them learn by experience, rather than by explanation.) When you next go through the book, encourage the child to read the words and sentences under the illustrations.

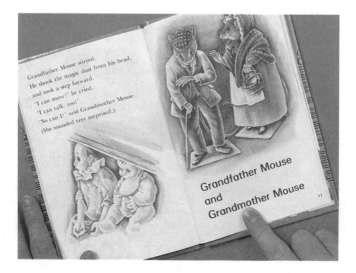

Don't rush in with the word before he* has time to think, but don't leave him floundering for too long. Always encourage him to feel that he is reading successfully, praising him when he does well, and avoiding criticism.

Now turn back to the beginning, and print the child's name in the space on the title page, using ordinary, not capital letters. Let him watch you print it: this is another useful experience.

*Children enjoy hearing the same story many times. Read this one as often as the child likes hearing it. The more opportunities he has of looking at the illustrations and **reading** the captions with you, the more he will come to recognise the words. Don't worry if he **remembers** rather than **reads** the captions. This is a normal stage in learning.*

If you have a number of books, let him choose which story he would like to have again.

**Footnote:* In order to avoid the continual "he or she", "him or her", the child is referred to in this book as "he". However, the stories are equally appropriate to girls and boys.

*Ask the child
to read the words,
using the pictures
to help him.*

Mrs
Pitter-Patter

the Griffle

the Griffle's tail

40

Mr Gotobed

window

bed

Look at these pictures together and then ask the child: "What is happening in this picture?"

What is happening in this picture?

Puddle Lane Reading Programme   Stage 1

There are several books at this Stage about the same characters. All the books at each Stage are separate stories and are written at the same reading level.
The lists below show other titles available at Stages 1 and 2.

Stage 1

1 Tim Catchamouse

2 Tessa and the Magician

3 The magic box

4 Mrs Pitter-Patter and the Magician

5 The vanishing monster

6 The Wideawake Mice

from The Wideawake Mice